THE MYSTERY ISSUE:

Where we peek behind the scenes, brave the unknown, and follow a myriad of curiosities...!

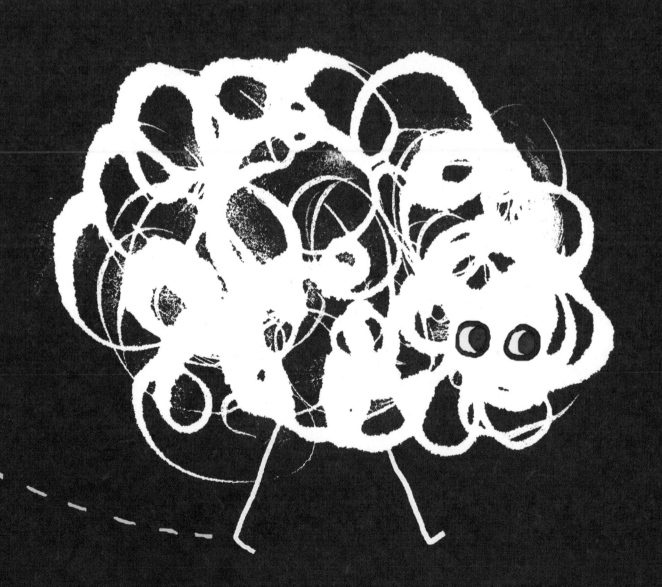

FROM US TO YOU:

the MYSTERY issue

OUR CONTRIBUTORS ANSWER A POLL:
DESCRIBE AN EXPERIENCE FROM THE PAST
THAT YOU FOUND MYSTIFYING.

pg. 52

CHARLOTTE AGER

I remember having close encounters with robins when it was summer and because my mum told me they were a winter bird, I was convinced I was a robin whisperer, and they were coming near me to tell me a secret.

pg. 28

YULIA DROBOVA

When we were little, we used to put two lumps of sugar in the closet at night to give the gnomes (that we imagined were living with us) a treat.

In the morning when we saw that the sugar was gone, we thought the gnomes were eating the sugar! Of course, it was just our dad putting it away after we had gone to sleep.

pg. 33

JIM PLUK

In my hometown, Bucaramanga, Colombia, I walked from the kitchen to the living room window and lingered, observing the view. It was a calm, quiet Sunday. Suddenly, I saw a silver object floating in the sky.

I was on the fifth floor and the ship was slightly above. I could see it clearly, it was big. It was silver, in the shape of two inverted bowls joined together, with orange, yellow, and green lights.

It floated for a moment and suddenly made a zigzag movement, leaving at an impressive speed. I didn't see where it went.

pg. 12

SIMONE REA

I happened to see something in the sky that was moving very fast creating straight lines. It looked like a star joining dots in the starry sky.

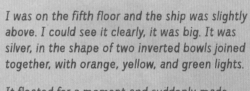

After all this time, I cannot imagine it was anything other than a UFO.

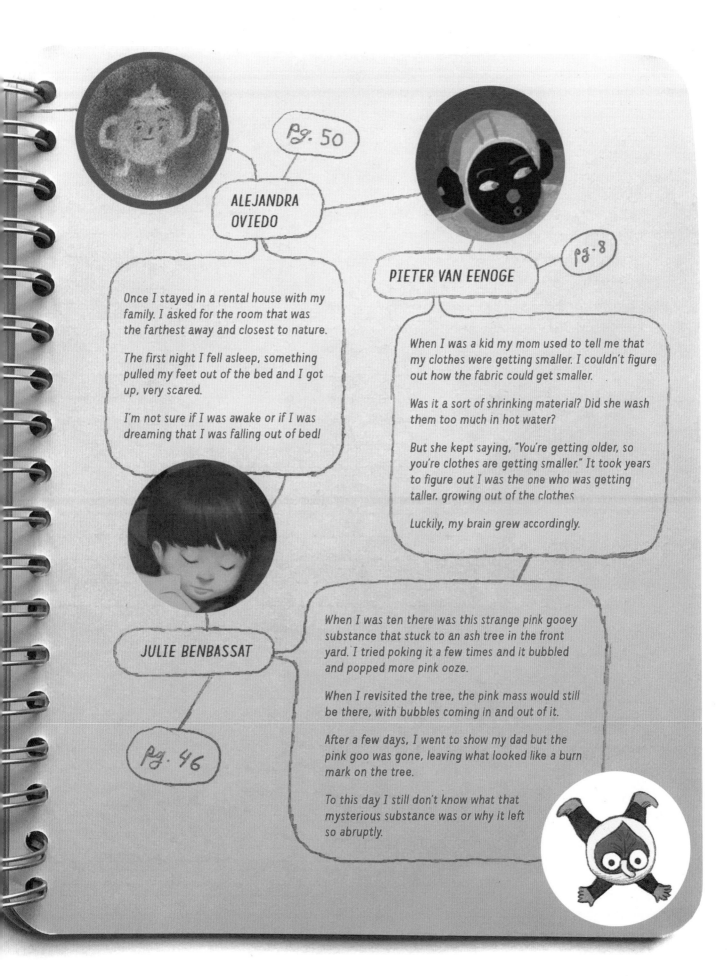

Pg. 50

ALEJANDRA OVIEDO

pg. 8

PIETER VAN EENOGE

Once I stayed in a rental house with my family. I asked for the room that was the farthest away and closest to nature.

The first night I fell asleep, something pulled my feet out of the bed and I got up, very scared.

I'm not sure if I was awake or if I was dreaming that I was falling out of bed!

When I was a kid my mom used to tell me that my clothes were getting smaller. I couldn't figure out how the fabric could get smaller.

Was it a sort of shrinking material? Did she wash them too much in hot water?

But she kept saying, "You're getting older, so you're clothes are getting smaller." It took years to figure out I was the one who was getting taller, growing out of the clothes

Luckily, my brain grew accordingly.

JULIE BENBASSAT

Pg. 46

When I was ten there was this strange pink gooey substance that stuck to an ash tree in the front yard. I tried poking it a few times and it bubbled and popped more pink ooze.

When I revisited the tree, the pink mass would still be there, with bubbles coming in and out of it.

After a few days, I went to show my dad but the pink goo was gone, leaving what looked like a burn mark on the tree.

To this day I still don't know what that mysterious substance was or why it left so abruptly.

inside

iLLUSTORiA

MEET SPECIAL GUESTS

LAUGH AND PLAY

READ AND LEARN

IN THIS ISSUE

guest curator
ISABEL ROXAS

guest writer
MATTHEW BURGESS

Our guest curator invites
four new artists to present:

**AYA KAKEDA
CHIA-CHI YU
CECILIA RUIZ
AL RODIN**

Visit page 20 to join the ride!

Chapter page art by:

typographic artist
EMILY RASMUSSEN

GRAB A FRIEND & TRY THESE!

ILLUSTORIA IS THE
OFFICIAL PUBLICATION
OF THE INTERNATIONAL
ALLIANCE OF YOUTH
WRITING CENTERS

TALKING HANDS

BY JASON STURGILL

What can jump higher than a building?

Is it some type of animal?

Anything that can jump, buildings can't jump!

HAHAHAHAHA

CHAPTER 1

Laugh and Play

OUR CHAPTER PAGES IN THIS ISSUE FEATURE TYPOGRAPHICAL ART BY EMILY RASMUSSEN.

WORD SLEUTH

```
O E M L L N O K T W
M L U A Z O J G T B
Y Z R U G Z D E Q E
S O D B H I R S L S
T O N Z A C C D U Y
I B U I E F D A Y X
F M N S N I F L L W
Y A O Z R E D L V Z
Q B C P U Z Z L E P
```

Flip to page 64 for the answer key.

by Pieter Van Eenoge

puzzle   riddle   baffle   mystify
conundrum   secret   bamboozle   magical

Laugh and play

SMALL TALK

WHAT DO YOU CALL AN ALLIGATOR WHO WORKS FOR A DETECTIVE AGENCY?

A PRIVATE INVESTI-GATOR

P.i.

JOKES!

WHY DID THE DETECTIVE WEAR A CAT COSTUME ON THE JOB?

BECAUSE HE WAS IN PURRR-SUIT

WHY DID THE DETECTIVE GET SUSPICIOUS ABOUT THE LOCAL SEAFOOD RESTAURANT?

SOMETHING SMELLED FISHY

A DETECTIVE SHOWED UP AT MY HOUSE AND ASKED:

WHERE WERE YOU BETWEEN 5 AND 6?

AND I ANSWERED...

IN KINDER-GARTEN!

BY JULIA McNAMARA

THE MYSTERY OF ZEBRA STRIPES!

Why do Zebras have stripes? Thanks to one creative biologist, the mystery is solved!

Do stripes help them regulate their temperature?

Do stripes make it easier for them to recognize each other?

HI!

HI BOB!

Are their stripes camouflage? What do you think?

For 10 years, a wildlife biologist named Tim Caro studied zebras in Tanzania to help solve the mystery. He made life-size zebra shapes out of wood and painted them with different kinds of markings.

HMMM...

Tim and his team observed the cutouts day and night to see if their stripes served as camouflage at different times of day. What did they discover? Zebras are really, really easy to see.

It's been known for some time that biting flies are confused by stripes. The flies are so dazed by stripes that they have a hard time landing. Tim's hunch was that a zebra's stripes keep them from being bitten by blood-sucking flies, because the flies can't land on them.

To test this, Tim turned himself into a zebra, by wearing a specially made zebra-striped suit. He roamed around zebra territory and counted how many flies landed on him. The answer? Not many!

Mystery solved! Besides being beautiful to look at, a zebra's stripes help protect them from biting flies and the diseases they carry.

SAY WHAT!?

WHAT ARE THESE CHARACTERS SAYING?

art by Simone Rea

When in doubt, stand still and wag your tail.

If something's boring, bring the party with you!

When embarrassed, some people are known to blush orange.

It's not the destination but the journey. Except if it's too dark to see anything.

What is always the biggest room in the house? The room for improvement.

MATCH THE SPEECH BUBBLE TO THE IMAGE & WRITE YOUR OWN ANSWER IN THE BLANK ONE

Laugh and play

THE SECRET LANGUAGE OF INSECTS

words by AMY SUMERTON *art by* KATE SAMWORTH

INSTRUCTIONS

Learn about the curious communication habits of a few insects, and then create your own insect dialogue with our story starter cards!

COMMUNICATION is the exchange of information between individuals: the transmitter and the receiver. For insects, it's an inborn mechanism. Each insect has a specific vocabulary that is truly distinct.

DIALOGUE is the conversation between characters in a novel, drama, and so on. Writers use dialogue to let characters speak (literally) in their own voices, imparting all kinds of information, feelings, fears, quirks, and more.

UNUSUAL INSECT COMMUNICATION

DOMINO CUCKOO BEE These bees lay their eggs in the nests of other bees!

FIREFLY Fireflies use the chemical process of bioluminescence (bodies that can make light) to find mates.

JAPANESE OWL MOTH These moths communicate using body color patterns. Their intricate designs fool predators into staying away.

ALIEN HEAD CICADA These cicadas produce an extremely LOUD song by rapidly buckling and unbuckling membranes in their abdomens.

OBSERVATION QUESTIONS

TO PLAY: Cut out the four cards on the opposite page.

1. Look through the Unusual Insect Communication above.

2. Stare intently into the eyes of the insects on each card. What are they communicating? What are their feelings, fears, and quirks?

3. Using the speech bubbles on the opposite side of the card, write an imagined conversation between these fascinating creatures.

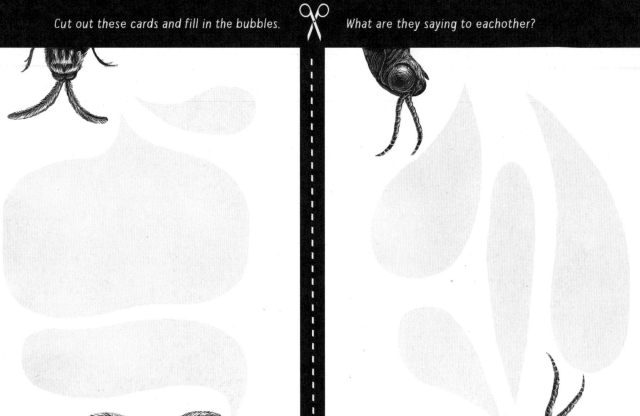

Do insects gossip? Do they philosophize? Are they singing?

MARTIAN MAZE

ENTER   EXIT

BY JESSE JACOBS

Laugh and play

TALKING HANDS

BY JASON STURGILL

@JGSPDX

CHAPTER 2

Read and Learn

TYPOGRAPHICAL ART BY EMILY RASMUSSEN.

WHY DOES THE OCEAN SOMETIMES GLEAM AT NIGHT?

Stars above and stars below
we stand within the starry glow

floating in this in-between,
a phosphorescent shimmering.

CABINET OF WONDERS

Guest curator **Isabel Roxas** and poet **Matthew Burgess** team up with four artists to reflect on mysteries that have captivated them since childhood.

AYA KAKEDA was born and raised in Tokyo, and has produced art for books, products, magazines, posters, and store installations for people all over the world.

CECILIA RUIZ is an author, illustrator, and designer originally from Mexico City. She now lives in Brooklyn, New York, teaching design and illustration at Queens College and the School of Visual Arts.

ISABEL ROXAS is an author and illustrator of books for young readers. Originally from Manila, she is now based in New York City, completing the third installment of her graphic novel series The Adventures of Team Pom.

CHIA-CHI YU is an illustrator based in Taiwan, after graduating from the National Art School in France. She loves using mixed materials and creating interesting illustrations.

AL RODIN is an award winning writer and illustrator from London, UK. His next book, *An Adventure for Lia and Lion*, will be published in May 2023.

MATTHEW BURGESS is a poet, professor, and children's book author who lives in Brooklyn and Berlin. His next book is *The Red Tin Box*, illustrated by Evan Turk.

art by Isabel Roxas

poetry by Matthew Burgess

HOW DO FLYING SQUIRRELS FLY?

Birds have wings and fish have fins
and dancers point their toes to spin,

but flying squirrels ride the wind—
they dare to soar with just their skin!

art by Aya Kakeda

WHAT SECRETS DO TREES TELL ONE ANOTHER?

Talking roots and fungi friends
grow and reach and breathe and bend—

a conversation underground
we've just begun to comprehend.

art by Chia-Chi Yu

WHY DO WE GET GOOSEBUMPS WHEN WE LISTEN TO BEAUTIFUL MUSIC?

I wonder where the music goes between my ears and tippy-toes?

Some inner river curves and flows to make the goose-bumps blossom so.

art by Cecilia Ruiz

ARE YOU THINKING WHAT
I THINK YOU'RE THINKING?

Each of us is in our skin.
Our thoughts are sprouting from within.

We read & draw & bloom our thoughts
of blizzards, bears, and astronauts...

But could we, *maybe*, in a blink,
glimpse the thoughts that others think?

art by Al Rodin

WE ASKED A POET...

ANIS MOJGANI IS OREGON'S POET LAUREATE.
WE GAVE HIM AN ARTICLE ABOUT DARK MATTER
BY ASTRO-PHYSICIST NEIL DEGRASSE TYSON.
ANIS RESPONDS TO THESE MYSTERIES OF SPACE:

Have you heard of *dark matter*? It's called "dark" because we literally don't know anything about it, except that it might exist and if it does there's a lot of it. Here's what we know: dark matter doesn't absorb reflect or emit electromagnetic waves which are everywhere all the time. Which means you can't see it, smell it, tickle it, or taste dark matter.

So if it were an ice cream, you could eat as much as you wanted and you wouldn't even feel it.

But, I guess what would be the point of eating ice cream you can't taste? Except you could taste the parts of it that weren't dark matter—sugar, creamy stuff, chocolate or strawberries, which are all delicious, so maybe dark matter ice cream wouldn't be so bad.

Guess what? Even though dark matter can't be seen, scientists believe it accounts for EIGHTY FIVE PERCENT of the universe.

That's a lot.

PHOTO BY FELIX MITTERMEIER

Like if the universe was actually an ice cream cone, dark matter would be MOST of the ice cream and only the TIP of the cone would be all that we know—the plants, every animal, every person you know, every stranger, all the oceans, all the air, every planet, every solar system, every single star—ALL of it would be the ice cream cone's last two bites.

And the rest of the cone and scoops would all be dark matter.

That's a lot of dark matter.
That's a lot of ice cream.

ANIS →

DARK MATTER

LIFE →

(UNSCIENTIFIC) DIAGRAM

read and learn

WHAT IS IT ?

BY YULIA DROBOVA

We have heard of this thing. What is it?

How long is it? Does it stretch?

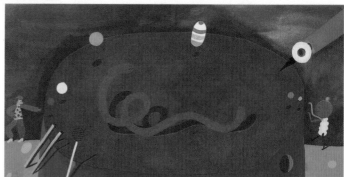

What is the sound that it makes?

Where is its face? Does it have expressions?

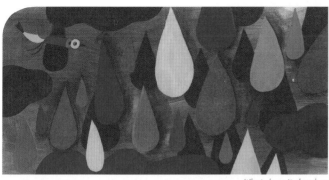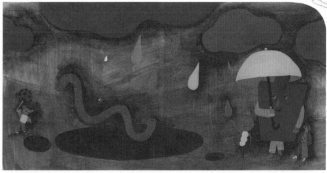

What does it do when the rains come?

What does it do when the sun shines?

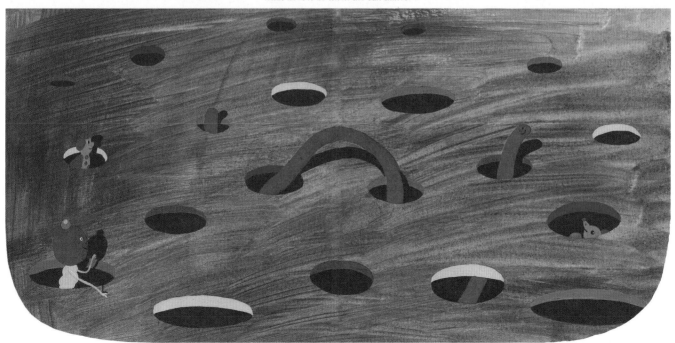

Where does it live? What shall we name it?

read and learn

Johannes is a free dog, a fast dog — such a fast dog!

THE EYES &
THE IMPOSSIBLE

DAVE EGGERS

DELUXE WOOD-BOUND HARDCOVER
COMING MAY 09, 2023 FROM McSWEENEY'S.
FIND IT AT YOUR LOCAL BOOKSTORE OR
STORE.MCSWEENEYS.NET.

THE EYES
& THE
IMPOSSIBLE

DAVE EGGERS

TRADITIONAL HARDCOVER COMING MAY 09, 2023
FROM KNOPF BOOKS FOR YOUNG READERS.

In this timeless story
by Dave Eggers, Johannes must run
faster, see better, and ultimately do more
than run and see — he must liberate
the ones he loves.

HAVE YOU EVER WANTED TO WRITE AND ILLUSTRATE YOUR OWN **PICTURE BOOK?**

what are you waiting for?

32 blank pages

13" x 13"

hardback cover

imagine your art here

MAKE YOUR OWN BOOK:
Write a story.
Draw the characters.
Work with a friend
or by yourself.
Draft it on scrap paper
first, get it just right,
then put it down in
your own beautiful
hardback book!

FIND IT AT:
STORE.MCSWEENEYS.NET

Freshta is an activist, author, mentor, and voice for those who are not able to share their stories. She is a refugee from Kabul, Afghanistan and now lives in Grand Rapids, Michigan.

YOUTH activist

"DON'T ALLOW OTHERS' DOUBTS TO STOP YOU FROM DOING BIG THINGS."

FRESHTA TORI JAN

Get her book, *I, Witness: Courage*, a memoir for middle grade readers about her persecution in Afghanistan as a child and her journey to the United States as a teen.

TELL US ABOUT YOUR RECENT PROJECT AND YOUR ACTIVIST WORK.

I am in the early stages of setting the groundwork of an organization to help Afghan women use their skills in sewing and crafting to make an income while they adjust to life in the US.

I, WITNESS

COURAGE

My Story of Persecution

FRESHTA TORI JAN

DO YOU HAVE ANY ADVICE FOR YOUNG ACTIVISTS?

You may be young, but you are just as powerful, bright, and brave as any adult or leader that you know. Don't allow others' doubt or opinion about your age stop you from doing big things.

FRESHTA WAS BRIEFLY REUNITED WITH HER FAMILY AT A REFUGEE CAMP IN NEW JERSEY AFTER EVACUATION FROM KABUL.

PHOTO BY TIM VANBEEK.

DEEP THOUGHTS
BY JIM PLUK

WOAH! WHAT IS THAT?!

A U.F.O.?!

DID YOU HEAR ABOUT WHAT THE HEAD* OF N.A.S.A. SAID?

NOPE.

HE SAID ** THAT THEY HAVE MYSTERIOUS PHOTOS OF UNCERTAIN OBJECTS WHICH NO PILOT OR EXPERT CAN IDENTIFY!

—GASP—

I SUPPOSE U.F.O.S COULD BE MORE INTELLIGENT THAN US?!

WHAT IF THEY ARE SO ADVANCED!!! THAT THEY CAN READ MINDS?

IF SO, THEY WILL SEE THAT I ONLY THINK ABOUT EATING JUNK FOOD!

OH GOSH!! WHAT A DISAPPOINTMENT WE WILL BE TO THEM.

JIM PLUK

* NATIONAL AERONAUTICS AND SPACE ADMINISTRATION

** FLIP TO PAGE 65 FOR QUOTE & ARTICLE.

(read and learn)

interview with

OUR COVER ARTIST
CÁTIA CHIEN:

Cátia Chien is a Brazilian-Tawainese children's book illustrator from São Paulo, Brazil. She is currently working in New York City. She is an award-winning illustrator and has created concept work for two animated films.

Q: DESCRIBE AN UNUSUAL OBJECT IN YOUR STUDIO.

A: Two items: a lint roller, which I use to pick up eraser shavings from my table, and a felt sculpture of Bear, from my book *The Bear and the Moon*. The sculpture of Bear was made by felt artist Victor Dubrovsky. It is one of my most prized possessions. I love it so much.

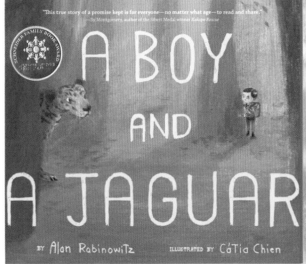

Q: TELL US ABOUT A DREAM PROJECT IDEA.

A: I want to write/direct a feature stop motion animation about dreams and dreaming. And I also would love to design a children's experiential garden and play space a la Niki De Saint Phalle's Giardino dei Tarocchi.

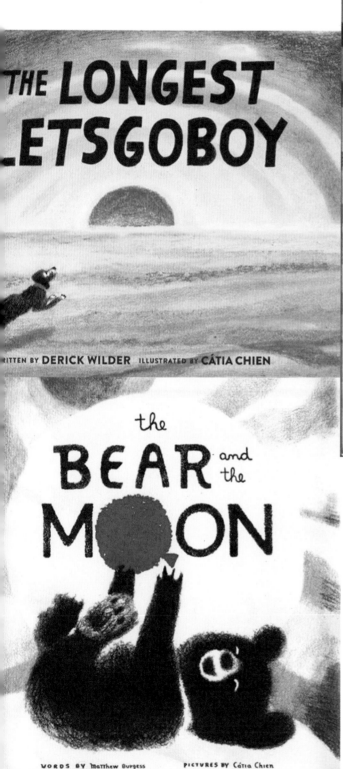

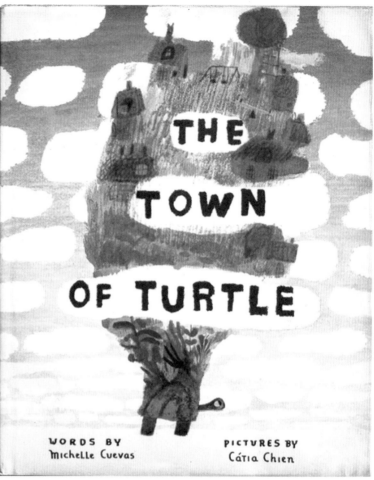

THE LONGEST LETSGOBOY

WRITTEN BY **DERICK WILDER** ILLUSTRATED BY **CÁTIA CHIEN**

the **BEAR** and the **MOON**

WORDS BY **Matthew Burgess** PICTURES BY **Cátia Chien**

↖ written by MATTHEW BURGESS, our guest writer on page 20

THE TOWN OF TURTLE

WORDS BY **Michelle Cuevas** PICTURES BY **Cátia Chien**

Q3 TELL US ABOUT A BOOK FROM CHILDHOOD THAT YOU CONNECTED WITH.

A3 I loved Mauricio de Sousa's Turma da Mônica comic series when I was little. As a bit of a proud odd duck myself, I identified with Mônica who was charming, sensitive, had big teeth, superhuman strength, and sported an unusual hairstyle for an 8 year old that some would call a comb over.

She's not your typical heroine and that is exactly why she captured so much of my imagination. I followed her neighborhood adventures with the rest of her friends as if they were my own. For a kid who moved around a lot these comics became my mainstay and it made me feel less alone.

(read and learn)

interview continued...

Q: FAVORITE SNACK WHILE WORKING?

A: Elephant ears, grapes, and olives.

← *from the book, THINGS TO DO, by Elaine Magliaro*

Q: WHAT'S NEXT, ON YOUR (ARTISTIC) PLATE?

A: I am illustrating a picture book called *Fireworks* written by Matthew Burgess and a bio picture book written by Minh Lê about Thích Nhất Hạnh.

Q: MORNING PERSON OR NIGHT OWL?

A: Morning person.

Q: ALBUM LISTENED TO RECENTLY?

A: *Industry Games* by Chika.

and when evening became night,
it glowed softly in the moonlight.

from THE BEAR AND THE MOON,
written by Matthew Burgess

(read and learn)

What's at the end of the rainbow?

A pot of gold?

The letter W!

That's rich!

@JGSPDX

CHAPTER 3

Draw, Write, Make

TYPOGRAPHICAL ART BY EMILY RASMUSSEN.

FIRST, BOIL AN EGG

TOAST THE BREAD

MASH UP THE AVOCADO AND SPREAD INTO THE SHAPE OF AN ALIEN'S HEAD!

SLICED EGG FOR EYES

TOMATO SLICE FOR MOUTH

OPTIONAL IDEAS:
- TRY THREE EYES
- ADD BASIL LEAVES FOR EARS
- USE A SLICED OLIVE FOR THE MOUTH FOR A SURPRISED EXPRESSION

mmmmm...

SERVE ON A PIECE OF SILVER FOIL SHAPED LIKE A FLYING SAUCER!

draw, write, make

MAKE THIS

D.I.Y. MYSTERY PANTRY!

YOU NEED:

SCRAP PAPER
GLUE STICK / TAPE
MARKERS, PENCILS
PANTRY ITEMS: CANS, JARS, TINS

CRUNCHY FUN

First, determine the goal of your edible item. Is it silly? Is it heart warming? Is it a surprise for April Fool's Day?

GMO FREE — Applause JUICE

CAN OF COMFORT — friendship flavor

LOW-SODIUM GLOOP

Write a few lists. Grab something from each to make your label. You'll need some adjectives, uplifting things, and types of edible items.

Bonus: make up your own brand name and logo to add.

less filling	STANDING OVATION	Juice
crunchy		Sauce
sugar free	HUG	Soup
dehydrated	AWESOME	Jerky
condensed	APPLAUSE	chips
xtra-salty!		Sprinkles
spicy	FUN	Gloop
organic	TOGETHER NESS	sludge

ECSTATIC VALLEY · organic · awesome SAUCE

Rainy day? Or you've got an accomplice to help? We challenge you to fill an entire shelf. Who will discover it later?

low sodium

★

GLOP

IMPORTED

APPLAUSE juice

星期日

awe-some SAUCE

DREAMS in a **JAR**

FIZZ-y **HUG** flavor SODA

8.45 FL OZ (250 ML)

EW

CONDENSED STANDING OVATION

COM-FORT SOUP

MIS-CHIEF

SPRI-NKLES

Use Carnation creamy results in and and baking recip

BITTER JOY

in stant CANNED ENTHU-SIASM

F IN

DEHYDRATED **TEARS**

draw, write, make

DRAW THIS → ## REBUS

A REBUS IS A PUZZLE MADE UP OF
LETTERS, PICTURES, AND SYMBOLS—AN
IDEA DATING BACK TO THE MIDDLE AGES.

SEE IF YOU CAN GUESS THE PHRASES
ON THESE VINTAGE BOTTLE CAPS.

--- This one translates:
"KEEP YOUR FINGERS CROSSED."

Think of some words that could be represented by a symbol or image.

LEAVE
FOR
BE
WHY
I
ARM
CHAIR
KNOWS

Try deciphering these images. What words do they stand for?

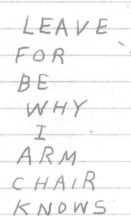

Try drawing images for these words. Add words in a row to make a phrase.

BELIEVE
(hint BEE + LEAF)

ARMCHAIR

WHY NOT (try KNOT)

LOVE YOU

Add or subtract a letter in order to use just part of a word-image.

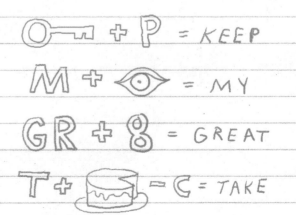

Try to guess these! Answers on page 65.

Five words for when you need someone to make up their mind.

Another way to say, "Hurry it up."

Five word phrase that involves being patient with unknowns.

A phrase that's another way of saying our theme: Mystery!

draw, write, make

CATEGORY-DEFYING MYSTERY CREATURES

words by Amy Sumerton *art by* Julie Benbassat

WELL HULLO!

Doc Anthurium here! In Issue 18: Rainforest, we looked at weird plants. This time, we focus on creatures that evade our attempts to categorize them.

In BIOLOGY (bio-life, ology-the study of), scientists use different word parts to name a creature based on its behavior and characteristics.

Here are some life forms that have made our job difficult!

Hagfish are important and confusing deep sea creatures. Also called slime eels, (although not eels), they belong to the class Agnatha (fish without jaws).

Hagfish lack scales and bones, yet have a skull made of cartilage. Their skin covers their bodies like a loose (super slimy) sock, and they have FOUR beating hearts. The loose skin helps them burrow into dead creatures... their main food!

Don't write off these scavengers as entirely gross; their feeding habits clean the sea floor.

So, perhaps we should call these HYDROTECHMORTILES...
(hydro-water, tech-craft, mort-death, ile-relating to, or capable of)?!

The pink glow worm is pink (and it does glow!) but it's not actually a worm—it's a Lampyridae—which means it's in the firefly and beetle family.

Pink glow worms are BIOLUMINESCENT (bio-life, lumin-light, escent-a developing action), like many Cnidaria (aquatic animals, such as jellyfish, coral, and anemones, and yup, you guessed it, fireflies!)

These amazing creatures are quite rare. You might spy one on a spring evening, crawling on the ground in southern California.

The green sea slug is a confounding creature: it appears to be part animal AND part plant. It's the first animal discovered to produce CHLOROPHYLL (*chloro-green, phyll-leaf*), a pigment found in plants.

They belong to the group Sacoglossa (sap-sucking sea slugs). Green sea slugs use CHLOROPLASTS (plasts-cells) from the algae they eat for PHOTOSYNTHESIS (photo-light, synthesis-combination). These "solar-powered" sea slugs can be found along the East Coast of North America.

NOW, YOU TRY!

Doc Anthurium's scientist friends have asked him to help categorize a newly discovered species.

Examine these traits, look through these word parts, draw the creature, and name it:

Micro.................Small	Hydro...............Water	Corp..................Body
Crypt...............To hide	Form.................Shape	Gastro............Stomach
Vor.....................To eat	Pod.....................Foot	Inter..............Between
Bi..........................Two	Omni...............Eats all	Auto.....................Self

OH GOSH!

_____

WHAT WOULD YOU NAME THIS CREATURE?

DRAW HERE

DRAWN BY YOU

PROMPT: Draw yourself as a secret agent.

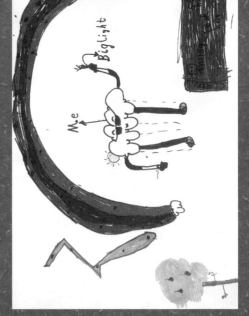

Reed, age 10,
New York, USA

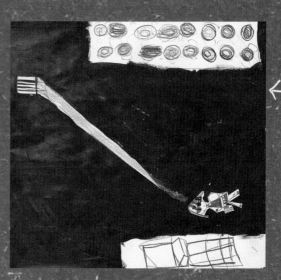

Sooyoung, age 8,
Washington, USA

cat headphones

Jetpack
floatily goo glasses

Miles, age 8,
Oregon, USA

Lucia, age 7, Canada

David,
age 7,
Canada

draw, write, make

WE ASKED STUDENTS TO WRITE A MYTH ABOUT THE ORIGIN OF THE MOON.

THE MOON SPEAKS

from FÁBRICA DE HISTORIAS in BUENOS AIRES, ARGENTINA
A MEMBER OF THE INTERNATIONAL ALLIANCE OF YOUTH WRITERS

written by LUISA DI BENEDETTO ITURBE, age 10
art by ALEJANDRA OVIEDO

Me preguntan de qué estoy hecha. No estoy hecha ni de queso, ni de rocas lunares. Estoy hecha de terciopelo. Tengo un campo de tulipanes en mi interior. Se cultiva cada partecita de adentro del tulipán para crear mi superficie tan suave como la parte fría de la almohada cuando le das vuelta.

Me parecen geniales las historias que se inventan, aunque la única verdad es la que les acabo de contar. Me siento suave sabiendo de dónde provengo. Es como una historia para dormir, con mi almohada dada vuelta. Ella me hace acordar de lo que estoy hecha. De mis campos de flores no me voy a olvidar.

They asked me what I'm made of. I'm not made of cheese, nor moon rocks. Rather, I am made of velvet. I have a tulips field inside me. Each little part is grown inside the tulip in order to create my smooth surface, just like the cool side of the pillow when you turn it 'round.

I think the stories that you guys all make up about me are great, although the only truth is the one I just told you. I feel soft knowing where I come from. It's just like a bedtime story, with my pillow turned around. It makes me remember what I'm made of. Of my field of flowers I will not forget.

draw, write, make

youth writing

WE ASKED STUDENTS TO WRITE A MYTH ABOUT THE ORIGIN OF THE MOON.

THE PERSISTENCE OF THE MOON

from LITTLE GREEN PIG *in* WHITEHAWK, BRIGHTON, UK
A MEMBER OF THE INTERNATIONAL ALLIANCE OF YOUTH WRITERS

written by ARCHIE HATTON, *age* 10
art by CHARLOTTE AGER

The Moon—so young, so arrogant—it wandered away
from T.M.A.*. It escaped, since it believed that finding
a planet to orbit was as boring as watching paint dry.
The Moon floated far from the Academy, each step
further into the Universe.

*The Moon Academy

"Hey, you! What are you doing here?
This is my turf!" said a mysterious planet.
"My name is Earth. Anyway, moons are a
waste of time. Get lost!"

That made the little Moon want to prove it wasn't a waste of time. First, it traveled to Saturn. No, too many other moons there. Neptune, too cold; Venus, too hot. Earth was the best out of all of them. Moon had to convince Earth! Moon danced, jumped, even made a cheesecake. None of this worked, until...

"Look, you're very annoying, but you're consistent. I'll let you orbit me on one condition – YOU STAY QUIET AND DO AS YOU ARE TOLD!" said the Earth.

"Yes," said the Moon joyfully, and then they lived happily ever after... except that's not always how it goes.

As the Moon had just begun to orbit, BOOM! The asteroid that wiped out the dinosaurs hit.

Just goes to show—you never know what is right around the corner, even (or especially) in Outer Space.

draw, write, make

A SERIES OF RIDDLES TALKING HANDS BY JASON STURGILL

CHAPTER 4

LOOK and LISTEN

TYPOGRAPHICAL ART BY EMILY RASMUSSEN.

Picked by
ISABEL ROXAS,
our guest curator
in this issue.

Frances Yip

discovery

EMI

This was actually a
promo album for the
airline Cathay Pacific
(my aunt was a flight
attendant), and I
loved it as a young(er)
person because it
introduced me to
new languages from
neighboring countries
in Southeast Asia.

FIND IT ON LAST.FM.

ON OUR DESK:

Selected by
our Editorial and
Marketing Manager,
CLAIRE ASTROW.

WATERCOLORS

I find painting to be so therapeutic
and meditative. Look for palettes that
have a built in mixing space, for ease.

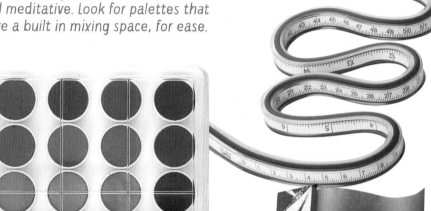

FLEXIBLE CURVE RULER

Draw squiggles
and curves!
Use it to create
abstract art or
repeat shapes
with precision.

SARAL TRANSFER PAPER

This paper is
a miracle for
transferring
images onto a
page in graphite.
Perfect for any
photo or drawing
you want to trace.

FAVORITE SNACK

Olives! They are
salty, delicious,
and beautiful.

Look and listen

COMIC BOOK REVIEW

with Bird and bird & House

hi

BUNNY AND TREE IS A STUNNING WORDLESS PICTURE BOOK BY BALINT ZSAKO.

(IT'S SO STUNNING, I ALMOST DON'T HAVE WORDS FOR IT, HAHAAA!)

A PORTRAIT OF A HIGHLY UNUSUAL FRIENDSHIP UNFOLDS.

A DETERMINED BUNNY TEAMS UP WITH A SHAPE-SHIFTING TREE.

OF ALL THINGS,

WHAT'S NEXT?

INCREDIBLE THINGS START HAPPENING. YOU'LL HAVE TO SEE IT TO BELIEVE IT.

AN EPIC ROADTRIP LEADS TO PLACES UNFAMILIAR.

WILL THEY FIND WHAT THEY ARE LOOKING FOR?

I READ THE WHOLE THING WITHOUT BLINKING— IT WAS THAT GOOD.

IT'S ONE OF THOSE BOOKS YOU'LL WANT TO KEEP ON YOUR BEDSIDE TABLE AND READ OVER AND OVER AGAIN. I JUST KNOW IT.

FIND THE BOOK AT ENCHANTEDLION.COM, OR YOUR LOCAL INDIE BOOKSTORE.

e.haidle

BROUGHT TO YOU BY CANDLEWICK STUDIO:

A POETIC TALE FOR AGES 4-6

WRITTEN BY DAVID ALMOND

ILLUSTRATED BY LAURA CARLIN →

THE WOMAN WHO TURNED CHILDREN INTO BIRDS

DAVID ALMOND
ILLUSTRATED BY
LAURA CARLIN

A RAUCOUS ROMP THROUGH LANGUAGE FOR AGES 4-8
- - -
BY ALEX LUBOMIRSKI

ILLUSTRATED BY CARLOS APONTE

WAHOO!

What are WORDS, Really?

written by Alexi Lubomirski   illustrated by Carlos Aponte

CANDLEWICK STUDIO
an imprint of Candlewick Press
www.candlewickstudio.com

*-by
DERECK WILDER
illustrated by
CÁTIA CHIEN*

*-published by
Chronicle Books*

Pure poetic
pondering about
pets loved and
lost.

How does love
reach beyond
time?

A must-read for
all pet lovers.

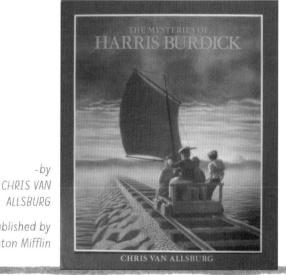

*-by
CHRIS VAN
ALLSBURG*

*-published by
Houghton Mifflin*

Ever imagine what you'd do if you were invisible?

A mysterious author leaves a
manuscript behind, containing
only images with titles. What
might the stories be?

Flip through this inventive
book in shades of green and
orange. As pages turn, some
images magically disappear.

*-by ALCIDES VILLAÇA and
ANDRÉS SANDOVAL*

-published by Tapioca Stories

Look and listen

ALIENS or Alienated?

PLUTO ROCKET
NEW IN TOWN

PAUL GILLIGAN

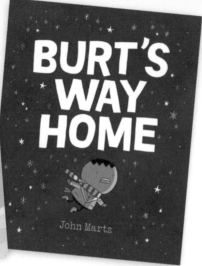

BURT'S WAY HOME

John Martz

Explore themes of self-discovery in these early graphic novels.

COPING WITH GRIEF AND LOSS

Explore themes of friendship, loss, and our connection with the natural world in these picture books.

RODNEY WAS A TORTOISE

NAN FORLER · YONG LING KANG

A Garden of Creatures

SHEILA HETI · ESMÉ SHAPIRO

tundra

FOR RESOURCES, INCLUDING DOWNLOADABLE MATERIALS, PLEASE VISIT TUNDRABOOKS.COM

EXCITING COMICS
from FLYING EYE BOOKS

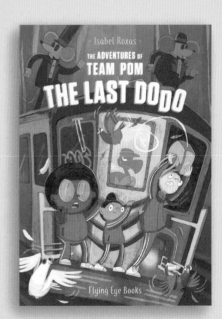

Juniper Mae: Knight of Tykotech City

From battling giant energy stealing robots to swimming around town with a giant squid to combat a pack of evil rats, we've got plenty of suspenseful stories to add to the shelf this season!

Whether you're looking to dive into a sci-fi world of futuristic technology and cute magical creatures, or laugh your way through the misadventures of a kooky crew of kids, there's a riddle for every age!

Team Pom: Squid Happens

Team Pom: The Last Dodo

Published by Flying Eye Books www.flyingeyebooks.com
@FlyingEyeBooks

Distributed by Penguin Random House Publisher Services
customerservice@penguinrandomhouse.com | 1-800-733-3000

Deeper Dive!

...CONTINUED FROM PAGE 9
CROSSWORD PUZZLE ANSWERS

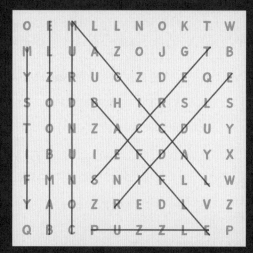

...CONTINUED FROM PAGE 14-15
SECRET LANGUAGE OF INSECTS

Additional tips for dialogue in your storytelling, by Amy Sumerton.

■ Add body language and setting. Sure, characters whisper, reply, ask, and say things. They also look out of windows, make sandwiches, sit down at messy tables, and rub their forehead.

■ Avoid small talk! Skip the unimportant stuff and stick to juicier conversations.

■ Say it out loud. Once you've written a scene with dialogue, act it out! Does it sound real and true?

■ Give each character a unique voice. People talk in many different ways! Make your characters stand out by developing HOW they talk. Punctuation for quotes is tricky!

■ Start a new paragraph when switching speakers, and separate a speaker's name from their speech with a comma. (For all the rules on dialogue punctuation, www.grammarist.com is a great resource.)

JAPANESE OWL MOTH

ALIEN-HEAD CICADA

PINK GLOWWORM

FROM "SECRET LANGUAGE OF INSECTS" BY AMY SUMERTON ON PAGE 14.

...CONTINUED FROM PAGE 11
FACTOIDS: WHY DO ZEBRAS HAVE STRIPES?

This age-old question has finally, definitively been answered by wildlife biologist, Tim Caro. Grab his book, *Zebra Stripes*, from your local library to hear about his experiments, including dressing up like a zebra and walking through lion-populated savannas in Tanzania.

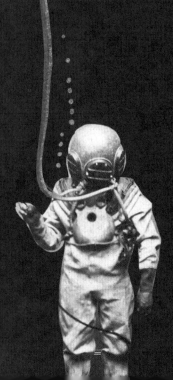

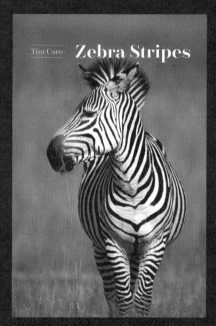

Tim Caro **Zebra Stripes**

BY WILDLIFE BIOLOGIST TIM CARO

...CONTINUED FROM PAGE 26-27
WE ASKED A POET

If you don't already know about the international treasure-trove of astrophysics that is Dr. Neil deGrasse Tyson, then we insist you get started investigating! Visit www.astronomy.com for stunning photos and grab his book at your local library branch, *Astrophysics for Young People in a Hurry*.

...CONTINUED FROM PAGE 33
UFO COMIC, BY JIM PLUK

This comic was inspired by an article on CNN Business, "NASA is getting serious about UFOs", written by Jackie Wattles, June 4, 2021. The full quote from the head of NASA, Bill Nelson, said "We don't know if it's extraterrestrial. We don't know if it's an enemy. We don't know if it's an optical phenomenon... And so, the bottom line is, we want to know."

...CONTINUED FROM PAGE 44-45
DRAW THIS: REBUS

A short history of the rebus: These riddles first emerged in the Middle Ages as a fanciful way to represent a family name or nickname. "Rebus" may have originated from the Latin phrase, *non verbis sed rebus*, meaning "not by words, but by things."

...CONTINUED FROM PAGE 45
ANSWERS TO REBUS PUZZLES

(clockwise from upper left)
1. Take it or leave it.
2. Make a beeline.
3. We'll have to wait and see.
4. No one knows for sure.

...CONTINUED FROM PAGE 46-47
CATEGORY-DEFYING MYSTERY CREATURES

Longing to hear more about these mysterious eels of the deep? Episode #8 of *Smologies*, a podcast by comedian Alie Ward, features an interview with Tim Winegard— professional hagfishologist (yes, it's a thing). Warning: detailed discussions about SLIME, in case that is a dealbreaker for you. Enjoy these bonus photos below.

A CLOSER LOOK AT A HAGFISH.

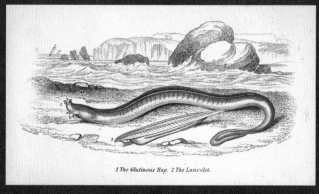

1 The Glutinous Hag. 2 The Lancelet.

YE OLDE ARTISTIC RENDERING OF A HAGFISH BY ROBERT HAMILTON, 1866.

CRABTREE A BOOK BY JON & TUCKER NICHOLS

ANYONE'S GUESS

Alfred Crabtree has no idea what this thing is.
Honestly? Neither do we.

VISIT

STORE. MCSWEENEYS. NET ← THIS IS WHERE TO FIND THE BOOK

to get your copy of *Crabtree*
and see if you can figure it out.

THIS IS ALFRED

THE YOUTH WRITING IN THIS ISSUE IS BY STUDENTS FROM:

Fábrica de Historias in Buenos Aires, Argentina and Little Green Pig in Brighton, UK.

TAKE A TRIP AND VISIT!

FIND A WRITING CENTER NEAR YOU: ▶ YOUTHWRITING.ORG

In every issue of *Illustoria*, students from the The International Alliance of Youth Writing Centers contribute their own writing and art to add a range of voices to these pages. The International Alliance is joined in a common belief that young people need places where they can write and be heard, where they can have their voices polished, published, and amplified. There are nearly seventy centers worldwide. Learn more at www.youthwriting.org.